Docker from Zero to Hero

The Complete Guide to Containerization & Deployment

Chapter 1: Introduction to Docker

What is Docker?

Docker is an open-source platform that enables developers to automate the deployment, scaling, and management of applications using containerization. Containers are lightweight, standalone, and executable packages that include everything needed to run a piece of software—code, runtime, libraries, and dependencies—ensuring that it runs consistently across different environments.

Docker simplifies application development by eliminating compatibility issues and making it easy to deploy applications across various computing environments. Whether you're working on a local machine, a cloud server, or an enterprise data center, Docker provides a seamless experience.

Why Use Docker?

1. Portability and Consistency

Docker ensures that an application runs identically in different environments, reducing the well-known "it works on my machine" problem. Since containers encapsulate all dependencies, there are no conflicts between different development and production setups.

2. Efficiency and Performance

Unlike traditional virtual machines (VMs), Docker containers share the host operating system's kernel, making them lightweight and fast. This leads to quicker start-up times and better resource utilization.

3. Scalability and Flexibility

Docker makes it easy to scale applications horizontally by running multiple containers in parallel. With tools like Docker Compose and Kubernetes, orchestrating complex, multi-container applications is simplified.

4. Simplified Deployment

Docker streamlines the CI/CD (Continuous Integration and Continuous Deployment) process, making it easy to test, deploy, and update applications across different environments.

5. Security and Isolation

Containers provide a secure environment by isolating applications and their dependencies. This reduces risks associated with conflicts and enhances security in multi-tenant environments.

Docker vs. Virtual Machines

Feature	Docker (Containers)	Virtual Machines (VMs)
Resource Usage	Lightweight, shares OS kernel	Heavy, requires full OS per instance
Start-up Time	Seconds	Minutes
Performance	Faster, less overhead	Slower due to OS virtualization
Portability	High, works across environments	Limited portability
Scalability	Easily scalable	Requires more resources

Docker provides a more efficient way to deploy applications compared to traditional virtual machines, making it the preferred choice for modern software development.

Installing Docker on Windows, macOS, and Linux

Before you can start using Docker, you need to install it on your system. Follow the steps below for your respective operating system.

Installing Docker on Windows

1. **Download Docker Desktop** from Docker's official website.
2. Run the installer and follow the setup instructions.
3. Enable **WSL 2 (Windows Subsystem for Linux 2)** during installation for optimal performance.
4. Restart your system after installation.
5. Open PowerShell or Command Prompt and verify installation by running:
6. `docker --version`

Installing Docker on macOS

1. **Download Docker Desktop** from Docker's official website.
2. Open the downloaded `.dmg` file and drag the Docker icon to the Applications folder.
3. Launch Docker from Applications and complete the setup.
4. Verify installation using:
5. `docker --version`

Installing Docker on Linux (Ubuntu/Debian)

1. Update your package index:
2. `sudo apt update`
3. Install necessary dependencies:
4. `sudo apt install apt-transport-https ca-certificates curl software-properties-common -y`
5. Add Docker's official GPG key:

6. ```
curl   -fsSL
https://download.docker.com/linux/ubuntu/gp
g | sudo   gpg   --dearmor   -o
/usr/share/keyrings/docker-archive-
keyring.gpg
```
7. Add Docker repository:
8. ```
echo "deb [arch=$(dpkg --print-architecture)
signed-by=/usr/share/keyrings/docker-
archive-keyring.gpg]
https://download.docker.com/linux/ubuntu
$(lsb_release  -cs)  stable"  |  sudo  tee
/etc/apt/sources.list.d/docker.list      >
/dev/null
```
9. Install Docker Engine:
10. ```
sudo apt update
```
11. ```
sudo  apt  install  docker-ce  docker-ce-cli
containerd.io -y
```
12. Verify installation:
13. ```
docker --version
```
14. (Optional) Add your user to the Docker group to avoid using `sudo`:
15. ```
sudo usermod -aG docker $USER
```

Log out and log back in for changes to take effect.

Post-Installation Test

After installing Docker, test your setup by running the **hello-world** container:

```
docker run hello-world
```

If Docker is installed correctly, you should see a message indicating that the Docker engine is running successfully.

Chapter 2: Understanding Docker Basics

Key Docker Concepts: Containers, Images, and Volumes

Before diving into hands-on usage, it's essential to understand some fundamental Docker concepts: **containers, images, and volumes**.

Containers

A **container** is a lightweight, standalone, and executable software package that includes everything needed to run an application: code, runtime, system tools, libraries, and settings. Containers ensure that software runs consistently across different environments, from development to production.

Images

A **Docker image** is a blueprint for creating a container. It is a pre-packaged application environment that includes all dependencies. Images are immutable, meaning they do not change once created. When a container runs, it does so based on an image.

Volumes

A **volume** is a persistent storage mechanism in Docker that allows data to be stored and shared between containers. Unlike the ephemeral storage of containers, volumes ensure that data persists even after a container stops or is removed.

Running Your First Container

Now that we understand the basic concepts, let's run our first container. The `docker run` command is used to create and start a container from an image.

```
docker run hello-world
```

This command pulls the `hello-world` image from Docker Hub (if not already available locally) and runs it as a container. You should see output indicating that Docker is working correctly.

Let's break down the command:

- `docker run` – Creates and starts a new container.
- `hello-world` – The name of the image being used.

To run an interactive container with a shell, try:

```
docker run -it ubuntu bash
```

This command does the following:

- `-it` – Runs the container in interactive mode.
- `ubuntu` – Uses the Ubuntu base image.
- `bash` – Starts a Bash shell inside the container.

You are now inside a running Ubuntu container and can execute commands as if using a regular Linux shell.

Exploring Docker Hub and Pulling Images

Docker Hub is a cloud-based repository where Docker images are stored and shared. To explore available images, visit Docker Hub.

To search for images from the command line, use:

```
docker search nginx
```

To pull an image locally before running a container, use:

```
docker pull nginx
```

Once downloaded, the image can be used to create containers.

Understanding `docker ps`, `docker stop`, and `docker rm`

Listing Running Containers (`docker ps`)

To check currently running containers, use:

```
docker ps
```

This command displays:

- **Container ID** – Unique identifier for the container.
- **Image** – The image used to create the container.
- **Command** – The command the container is executing.
- **Status** – Whether the container is running, stopped, etc.

To see all containers, including stopped ones, use:

```
docker ps -a
```

Stopping a Container (`docker stop`)

To stop a running container, use:

```
docker stop <container_id>
```

Replace `<container_id>` with the actual ID of the container (retrieved from `docker ps`).

Removing a Container (`docker rm`)

To remove a stopped container, use:

```
docker rm <container_id>
```

To remove multiple containers at once, use:

```
docker rm $(docker ps -aq)
```

This command removes all stopped containers.

Summary

- **Containers** are lightweight, portable execution environments.
- **Images** act as templates for creating containers.
- **Volumes** provide persistent storage.
- `docker run` starts a new container.
- Docker Hub is a repository for Docker images.
- `docker ps` lists running containers.
- `docker stop` stops a running container.
- `docker rm` removes a container.

With these basics covered, you're now ready to explore more advanced Docker functionalities in the next chapter!

Chapter 3: Docker Images and Dockerfiles

What are Docker Images?

Docker images are lightweight, standalone, and executable software packages that include everything needed to run an application: code, runtime, libraries, environment variables, and configurations. These images act as blueprints for creating Docker containers. Images are built in layers, which makes them efficient in storage and execution.

Key characteristics of Docker images:

- **Immutability:** Once an image is created, it remains unchanged.
- **Layered Structure:** Built from multiple layers, where each layer represents an instruction in the Dockerfile.
- **Portability:** Can be shared and run across different environments without modification.

Docker images are stored in registries like **Docker Hub**, **Amazon Elastic Container Registry (ECR)**, and **Google Container Registry (GCR)**. You can pull images from these registries and use them to create containers.

Creating a Dockerfile

A **Dockerfile** is a script-like text file that contains a set of instructions to build a Docker image. It defines everything required for the application to run.

Basic Structure of a Dockerfile

```
# Use an official base image
FROM node:18-alpine

# Set the working directory
WORKDIR /app

# Copy application files
COPY package.json .
COPY . .

# Install dependencies
RUN npm install

# Expose the application port
EXPOSE 3000

# Define the command to run the app
CMD ["npm", "start"]
```

Common Dockerfile Instructions

- **FROM:** Specifies the base image to use.
- **WORKDIR:** Sets the working directory inside the container.
- **COPY:** Copies files from the host system into the container.

- **RUN:** Executes commands inside the container during build.
- **EXPOSE:** Defines which ports will be available.
- **CMD:** Specifies the default command that runs when a container starts.

Building Custom Images (docker build)

Once a Dockerfile is created, you can build an image using the `docker build` command.

Building an Image

Run the following command in the same directory as your Dockerfile:

```
docker build -t my-app .
```

The `-t` flag assigns a tag (name) to the image. The dot (`.`) specifies the build context (current directory).

Listing Images

To see all locally stored Docker images, use:

```
docker images
```

Best Practices for Writing Dockerfiles

Writing efficient and optimized Dockerfiles is essential for performance and maintainability. Here are some best practices:

1. **Use Official Base Images**
   - Always start with minimal, verified, and secure base images (e.g., `node:alpine` instead of `node:latest`).
2. **Leverage Layer Caching**
   - Place frequently unchanged instructions (like `FROM` and `RUN apt-get install`) at the top.
3. **Reduce the Number of Layers**
   - Combine multiple commands in a single `RUN` instruction to minimize image layers:
4. `RUN apt-get update && apt-get install -y curl unzip && rm -rf /var/lib/apt/lists/*`
5. **Use .dockerignore**
   - Create a `.dockerignore` file to exclude unnecessary files and reduce image size.
6. `node_modules`
7. `.git`
8. `.env`
9. **Use Multi-Stage Builds**
   - Multi-stage builds help create leaner images by separating build dependencies from the final image.
10. `FROM golang:1.19 AS builder`
11. `WORKDIR /app`
12. `COPY . .`
13. `RUN go build -o main .`
14.

```
15.  FROM alpine:latest
16.  COPY --from=builder /app/main /
17.  CMD ["/main"]
```
18. Avoid Running Containers as Root
>   o Improve security by using a non-root user.
```
19.  RUN useradd -m appuser
20.  USER appuser
```

Optimizing Image Size

Smaller images lead to faster deployments and lower storage costs. Here's how to optimize image size:

- **Use Minimal Base Images:** Alpine-based images (e.g., `python:alpine`, `node:alpine`) are smaller than full Linux distributions.
- **Clean Up Unnecessary Files:** Remove unnecessary dependencies after installing packages.
- **Use Multi-Stage Builds:** Keep only the final, necessary artifacts in production images.
- **Compress Layers:** Reduce the number of `RUN` statements and combine commands where possible.
- **Avoid Including Debugging Tools:** Remove unnecessary tools and libraries before deploying.

By following these best practices, you can build efficient, secure, and optimized Docker images.

Chapter 4: Docker Networking

Default Networking Modes

Docker provides several built-in networking modes that define how containers communicate with each other and the external network. The default networking modes are:

1. Bridge Network (default)

- When a container is started without specifying a network, it is automatically connected to the default `bridge` network.
- Containers in the same bridge network can communicate with each other using their container names.
- The host machine can access the container using port mapping (`-p` option).

Example:

```
docker network ls  # List available networks
docker run -d --name my_container nginx  # Uses default bridge network
```

2. Host Network

- The container shares the network namespace of the host, meaning it directly uses the host's network stack.
- This mode removes network isolation, which can improve performance but reduces security.

Example:

```
docker run --network host nginx
```

3. None Network

- Completely disables networking for the container.
- Useful for security purposes or testing applications that do not require network access.

Example:

```
docker run --network none nginx
```

4. Overlay Network (Swarm mode)

- Used for multi-host networking in Docker Swarm.
- Allows services running on different hosts to communicate as if they are on the same local network.

Example:

```
docker    network    create    -d    overlay
my_overlay_network
```

5. Macvlan Network

- Assigns a unique MAC address to the container, making it appear as a physical device on the network.
- Useful for legacy applications that require direct network access.

Example:

```
docker network create -d macvlan --subnet=192.168.1.0/24 my_macvlan
```

Creating Custom Networks

Creating a custom network allows better control over container communication. The `bridge` network is most commonly used.

Create a Custom Bridge Network

```
docker network create my_custom_network
```

Run a Container in the Custom Network

```
docker run -d --name my_app --network my_custom_network nginx
```

Inspect a Network

```
docker network inspect my_custom_network
```

Connecting Multiple Containers

Containers can communicate within the same network by using their container names as hostnames.

Example: Running Two Containers in the Same Network

```
docker network create my_network
docker run -d --name db --network my_network
postgres
docker run -d --name app --network my_network
my_app_image
```

The `app` container can reach `db` using the hostname `db`.

Exposing and Publishing Ports

Docker allows exposing and mapping ports to enable external access.

Exposing Ports Internally

Containers can expose ports internally using the `EXPOSE` instruction in the `Dockerfile`.

```
EXPOSE 80
```

Publishing Ports with `-p`

The `-p` flag maps a container's internal port to a host port.

```
docker run -d -p 8080:80 nginx
```

- `8080:80` maps port `80` inside the container to port `8080` on the host.

Binding to a Specific IP Address

```
docker run -d -p 127.0.0.1:8080:80 nginx
```

This binds the container's port `80` to `127.0.0.1:8080`, making it accessible only from the local machine.

Summary

- Docker provides multiple networking modes (`bridge`, `host`, `none`, `overlay`, and `macvlan`).
- Custom networks allow better control over container communication.
- Containers in the same network can communicate using container names.
- Ports can be exposed using `EXPOSE` or published using `-p` for external access.

This chapter provides the foundation for understanding Docker networking, which is essential for deploying and managing containerized applications effectively.

Chapter 5: Docker Volumes and Persistent Storage

Containers are ephemeral by nature, meaning any data stored inside a container is lost when the container stops or is removed. To persist data and share it between containers, Docker provides **volumes** and **bind mounts**. In this chapter, we will explore these storage options, how to manage data between container restarts, and best practices for handling databases in containers.

Understanding Volumes and Bind Mounts

Volumes

Docker volumes are the preferred method for persisting data in containers because they are managed by Docker and provide better performance and security than bind mounts. Volumes are stored outside the container's filesystem in `/var/lib/docker/volumes/` and can be easily shared across multiple containers.

Creating and Using Volumes:

```
# Create a volume
docker volume create my_volume

# Run a container using the volume
```

```
docker     run     -d     --name     my_container     -v
my_volume:/app/data busybox

# Inspect volume details
docker volume inspect my_volume
```

Bind Mounts

Bind mounts allow you to link a specific directory on the host machine to a directory inside the container. Unlike volumes, bind mounts rely on the host system's filesystem, which means they are less portable and can pose security risks.

Example of Bind Mount Usage:

```
# Run a container with a bind mount
docker     run     -d     --name     my_container     -v
/host/path:/container/path busybox
```

Key Differences Between Volumes and Bind Mounts

Feature	Volumes	Bind Mounts
Managed by Docker	Yes	No
Stored in /var/lib/docker/volumes/	Yes	No
Can be backed up easily	Yes	No
Requires existing host directory	No	Yes
Works across multiple platforms	Yes	No

Managing Data Between Container Restarts

To ensure data persists across container restarts, you must use either volumes or bind mounts. When a container is removed, its anonymous volumes are deleted unless explicitly referenced.

Steps to Persist Data Across Restarts:

1. Create a named volume.
2. Mount the volume to a container.
3. Restart or remove the container without losing data.

```
# Create and run a container with a persistent
volume
docker run -d --name my_app -v my_data:/app/data
busybox

# Stop and remove the container
docker stop my_app
docker rm my_app

# Start a new container with the same volume
docker run -d --name my_app_new -v
my_data:/app/data busybox
```

Best Practices for Handling Databases in Containers

Running databases inside containers requires careful handling to avoid data loss and ensure high performance. Here are some best practices:

1. Always Use Volumes for Databases

Using volumes instead of bind mounts ensures better consistency and portability.

```
docker      run      -d      --name      mysql      -e
MYSQL_ROOT_PASSWORD=root                             -v
mysql_data:/var/lib/mysql mysql
```

2. Backup and Restore Data

Regular backups are crucial when running databases in containers.

```
# Backup MySQL database
docker   exec   mysql   mysqldump   -u   root   -
pROOT_PASSWORD mydb > backup.sql

# Restore MySQL database
cat backup.sql | docker exec -i mysql mysql -u
root -pROOT_PASSWORD mydb
```

3. Use `--tmpfs` for Temporary Data

If you need high-speed temporary storage, you can mount a tmpfs volume.

```
docker   run   -d   --tmpfs   /app/tmp:rw,size=100m
busybox
```

4. Manage Volume Lifecycle

Unused volumes can accumulate over time, so it's essential to clean them up periodically.

```
# List volumes
docker volume ls

# Remove a specific volume
docker volume rm my_volume

# Remove all unused volumes
docker volume prune
```

Conclusion

Understanding and properly managing Docker storage is key to maintaining persistent data across container restarts. Volumes are the preferred choice for most use cases, especially for databases, while bind mounts are useful when working with local files on the host system. By following best practices, you can ensure data integrity and optimal performance in your Dockerized applications.

Chapter 6: Docker Compose: Multi-Container Applications

What is Docker Compose?

Docker Compose is a tool that simplifies the management of multi-container Docker applications. Instead of manually running and linking multiple containers, Docker Compose allows you to define and manage them using a single configuration file called `docker-compose.yml`. This file describes the services, networks, and volumes your application needs, making it easier to deploy and maintain complex setups.

Key Features of Docker Compose:

- **Multi-container orchestration:** Easily define multiple services within a single file.
- **Service dependency management:** Automatically start services in the correct order.
- **Networking made simple:** Services communicate through an isolated Docker network.
- **Scalability:** Run multiple instances of a service using scaling options.
- **Consistent environments:** Use the same configuration for development, testing, and production.

Writing a `docker-compose.yml` File

A `docker-compose.yml` file is a YAML configuration file that defines the services, networks, and volumes for your application. Here's an example of a simple `docker-compose.yml` file for a web application with a database:

```
version: '3.8'

services:
  app:
    image: myapp:latest
    ports:
      - "5000:5000"
    depends_on:
      - db
    environment:
      -
DATABASE_URL=postgres://user:password@db:5432/myd
atabase

  db:
    image: postgres:15
    restart: always
    environment:
      POSTGRES_USER: user
      POSTGRES_PASSWORD: password
      POSTGRES_DB: mydatabase
    volumes:
      - db_data:/var/lib/postgresql/data

volumes:
  db_data:
```

Explanation:

- **services**: Defines different containers (app and db in this case).
- **app service**: Runs a web application and exposes port 5000.
- **db service**: Runs PostgreSQL and persists data using volumes.
- **depends_on**: Ensures that the db service starts before app.
- **volumes**: Ensures that database data is stored persistently.

Running Multiple Services with `docker-compose up`

Once you have a `docker-compose.yml` file, you can use `docker-compose` commands to manage your application.

Starting Services:

Run the following command to start all services defined in the file:

```
docker-compose up -d
```

The `-d` flag runs the services in detached mode (background).

Viewing Running Services:

```
docker-compose ps
```

This lists the currently running services.

Stopping Services:

```
docker-compose down
```

This stops and removes all running services.

Environment Variables and Configuration Management

Docker Compose allows you to define environment variables for better configuration management. You can use:

Inline Environment Variables:

```
environment:
  -
DATABASE_URL=postgres://user:password@db:5432/myd
atabase
```

.env File:

Instead of hardcoding secrets in the YAML file, you can use an .env file:

```
DATABASE_URL=postgres://user:password@db:5432/myd
atabase
```

Then reference it in docker-compose.yml:

```
environment:
  - DATABASE_URL=${DATABASE_URL}
```

Benefits of Using `.env`:

- Keeps sensitive data out of version control.
- Allows different configurations for development, testing, and production.

By using Docker Compose, you can streamline multi-container application management, making deployment and scaling more efficient.

Chapter 7: Working with Docker Registries

7.1 Introduction to Docker Registries

Docker registries are repositories where container images are stored, managed, and shared. They enable developers and organizations to distribute containerized applications efficiently. The most commonly used public registry is **Docker Hub**, but private registries and cloud-based registries like **Amazon Elastic Container Registry (ECR), Google Container Registry (GCR), and GitHub Container Registry (GHCR)** offer additional features and security benefits.

In this chapter, we will cover:

- Pushing and pulling images to Docker Hub
- Setting up a private Docker registry
- Using cloud-based registries like Amazon ECR, Google Container Registry, and GitHub Container Registry

7.2 Pushing and Pulling Images to Docker Hub

Docker Hub is the default and most widely used container registry. It allows users to store, distribute, and manage Docker images.

7.2.1 Logging into Docker Hub

Before you can push images to Docker Hub, you need to log in:

```
docker login
```

You'll be prompted to enter your **Docker Hub username** and **password**.

7.2.2 Pulling an Image from Docker Hub

To pull an image from Docker Hub, use the following command:

```
docker pull <image-name>
```

For example, to pull the official **Nginx** image:

```
docker pull nginx
```

7.2.3 Tagging an Image

Before pushing an image to Docker Hub, you need to tag it with your Docker Hub repository name:

```
docker    tag    <local-image-id>    <dockerhub-username>/<repository-name>:<tag>
```

Example:

```
docker tag my-app mydockerhubuser/my-app:latest
```

7.2.4 Pushing an Image to Docker Hub

Once an image is tagged, push it to Docker Hub using:

```
docker    push    <dockerhub-username>/<repository-
name>:<tag>
```

Example:

```
docker push mydockerhubuser/my-app:latest
```

7.3 Setting Up a Private Docker Registry

If you prefer to store your images privately, you can set up your own **Docker registry**.

7.3.1 Running a Local Docker Registry

Docker provides an official **registry** image that you can run locally:

```
docker    run    -d   -p   5000:5000    --name    registry
registry:2
```

This will start a local registry accessible on **http://localhost:5000**.

7.3.2 Tagging and Pushing an Image to Your Private Registry

You need to tag your image with the local registry URL before pushing it:

```
docker tag my-app localhost:5000/my-app
```

Push the image to the private registry:

```
docker push localhost:5000/my-app
```

To pull the image from your private registry:

```
docker pull localhost:5000/my-app
```

7.4 Using Cloud-Based Registries

Many cloud providers offer container registries with additional security and scalability. Below, we cover how to use **Amazon Elastic Container Registry (ECR), Google Container Registry (GCR), and GitHub Container Registry (GHCR).**

7.4.1 Amazon Elastic Container Registry (ECR)

Amazon ECR is a managed container registry service provided by AWS.

7.4.1.1 Authenticating to ECR

First, configure AWS CLI and authenticate:

```
aws ecr get-login-password --region <your-region>
| docker login --username AWS --password-stdin
<aws-account-id>.dkr.ecr.<region>.amazonaws.com
```

7.4.1.2 Creating an ECR Repository

```
aws ecr create-repository --repository-name my-app
```

7.4.1.3 Tagging, Pushing, and Pulling an Image

```
docker      tag      my-app      <aws-account-
id>.dkr.ecr.<region>.amazonaws.com/my-app
docker          push          <aws-account-
id>.dkr.ecr.<region>.amazonaws.com/my-app
```

To pull the image:

```
docker            pull            <aws-account-
id>.dkr.ecr.<region>.amazonaws.com/my-app
```

7.4.2 Google Container Registry (GCR)

Google Container Registry (GCR) is Google Cloud's managed container registry.

7.4.2.1 Authenticating to GCR

```
gcloud auth configure-docker
```

7.4.2.2 Tagging, Pushing, and Pulling an Image

```
docker tag my-app gcr.io/<project-id>/my-app
docker push gcr.io/<project-id>/my-app
```

To pull the image:

```
docker pull gcr.io/<project-id>/my-app
```

7.4.3 GitHub Container Registry (GHCR)

GitHub provides a container registry integrated with GitHub Actions and repositories.

7.4.3.1 Authenticating to GHCR

```
echo <github-token> | docker login ghcr.io -u
<github-username> --password-stdin
```

7.4.3.2 Tagging, Pushing, and Pulling an Image

```
docker tag my-app ghcr.io/<github-username>/my-
app:latest
docker push ghcr.io/<github-username>/my-
app:latest
```

To pull the image:

```
docker pull ghcr.io/<github-username>/my-
app:latest
```

7.5 Conclusion

This chapter covered how to work with Docker registries, including:

- Pushing and pulling images to/from Docker Hub
- Setting up a private Docker registry
- Using cloud-based registries like Amazon ECR, Google Container Registry, and GitHub Container Registry

Understanding how to efficiently store and distribute Docker images is crucial for managing containerized applications in real-world environments.

Chapter 8: Docker Security Best Practices

Running Containers with Least Privilege

One of the fundamental principles of security is the principle of least privilege. In the context of Docker, this means ensuring that containers run with only the permissions they need to function properly.

Best Practices:

- **Avoid Running as Root:** By default, Docker containers run as the root user, which can pose security risks if exploited. Instead, create a non-root user inside the container using a Dockerfile:
- `RUN adduser --disabled-password --gecos '' appuser`
- `USER appuser`
- **Use User Namespace Remapping:** Enable user namespace remapping to isolate the container's privileges from the host system.
- `"userns-remap": "default"`
- **Restrict Capabilities:** Reduce the number of Linux capabilities assigned to containers using the `--cap-drop` flag:

- ```
  docker      run      --cap-drop=ALL      --cap-
  add=NET_BIND_SERVICE myimage
  ```
- **Use Read-Only File Systems:** Prevent unintended modifications to files by mounting containers with a read-only file system:
- ```
  docker run --read-only myimage
  ```

Scanning Images for Vulnerabilities

Container images can contain security vulnerabilities, so it's essential to scan them before deployment.

Best Practices:

- **Use Image Scanning Tools:** Regularly scan images for vulnerabilities using tools like:
  - **Trivy:**
  - ```
    trivy image myimage
    ```
  - **Clair:** Integrate with CI/CD pipelines for continuous scanning.
  - **Docker Scout:** A built-in solution for vulnerability detection.
- **Use Minimal Base Images:** Choose lightweight, security-focused images such as Alpine or Distroless.
- **Regularly Update Images:** Pull the latest security-patched versions of images and rebuild containers.
- ```
  docker pull myimage:latest
  ```

Limiting Container Resources

Restricting CPU, memory, and other system resources prevents a single container from consuming all available host resources, reducing the risk of denial-of-service (DoS) attacks.

Best Practices:

- **Limit CPU Usage:**
- `docker run --cpus=1 myimage`
- **Restrict Memory Usage:**
- `docker run --memory=512m --memory-swap=1g myimage`
- **Control I/O Operations:** Limit disk I/O using `--blkio-weight`:
- `docker run --blkio-weight=500 myimage`
- **Set Restart Policies Carefully:** Avoid using `--restart=always`, which can lead to unintended container reboots.

Avoiding Common Security Pitfalls

There are several common misconfigurations that can make Docker environments vulnerable.

Best Practices:

- **Do Not Expose the Docker Daemon Socket:** Never mount `/var/run/docker.sock` inside containers unless absolutely necessary.

- **Use Secrets Management:** Avoid storing secrets in environment variables. Instead, use Docker Secrets or external secret management solutions like Vault.
- ```
  echo "mysecret" | docker secret create
  my_secret -
  ```
- **Restrict Network Access:** Use network policies to limit inter-container communication.
- ```
  docker network create --
  subnet=192.168.1.0/24 my_secure_network
  ```
- **Enable Logging and Monitoring:** Implement centralized logging using tools like Fluentd, Loki, or ELK Stack to detect suspicious activity.
- **Keep Docker Updated:** Regularly update Docker Engine and its dependencies to protect against known vulnerabilities.
- ```
  sudo apt update && sudo apt upgrade docker-
  ce
  ```

By following these security best practices, you can significantly reduce the attack surface of your Dockerized applications and ensure a safer containerized environment.
  ```

Chapter 9: Introduction to Kubernetes

What is Kubernetes, and Why is it Important?

Kubernetes, often abbreviated as K8s, is an open-source container orchestration platform designed to automate the deployment, scaling, and management of containerized applications. Originally developed by Google and now maintained by the Cloud Native Computing Foundation (CNCF), Kubernetes has become the industry standard for container orchestration.

Why Kubernetes Matters

- **Scalability**: Kubernetes efficiently scales applications up or down based on demand.
- **Automation**: Handles deployment, rollback, and monitoring automatically.
- **Self-Healing**: Restarts failed containers and replaces unresponsive nodes.
- **Load Balancing**: Distributes traffic to ensure optimal performance.
- **Portability**: Works across on-premise and cloud environments.

Deploying Docker Containers on Kubernetes

Before deploying containers on Kubernetes, you must have a working Kubernetes cluster. This can be set up using tools like Minikube (for local testing) or cloud-managed Kubernetes services like Google Kubernetes Engine (GKE), Amazon EKS, or Azure AKS.

Steps to Deploy a Docker Container on Kubernetes

1. **Create a Docker Image**
   - Write a `Dockerfile` and build your image.
   - Push the image to a container registry (Docker Hub, AWS ECR, GCR, etc.).
2. **Define a Kubernetes Deployment**
   - Use a YAML file to specify the deployment configuration.
   - Example:
   - `apiVersion: apps/v1`
   - `kind: Deployment`
   - `metadata:`
   -   `name: my-app`
   - `spec:`
   -   `replicas: 3`
   -   `selector:`
   -     `matchLabels:`
   -       `app: my-app`
   -   `template:`
   -     `metadata:`
   -       `labels:`
   -         `app: my-app`
   -     `spec:`
   -       `containers:`

```
o            - name: my-app
o              image:           my-docker-
   image:latest
o                ports:
o                  - containerPort: 80
```
3. **Apply the Deployment**
```
4. kubectl apply -f deployment.yaml
```
5. **Expose the Application**
```
6. kubectl    expose    deployment    my-app    --
   type=LoadBalancer --port=80
```
7. **Verify the Deployment**
```
8. kubectl get pods
9. kubectl get services
```

Understanding Pods, Services, and Deployments

Pods

A **Pod** is the smallest deployable unit in Kubernetes and encapsulates one or more containers. Pods share networking and storage resources, making it easy to manage application components.

Services

A **Service** provides a stable endpoint to access Pods, ensuring reliable networking. Kubernetes Services handle load balancing and traffic routing, allowing seamless communication between applications.

Deployments

A **Deployment** is responsible for maintaining a specified number of running Pod replicas. Deployments manage updates, rollbacks, and scaling automatically.

Using Minikube to Test Locally

Minikube is a lightweight Kubernetes implementation that runs a cluster on a local machine. It is useful for testing Kubernetes applications before deploying to a cloud provider.

Setting Up Minikube

1. **Install Minikube**
2. ```
   curl                              -LO
   https://storage.googleapis.com/minikube/rel
   eases/latest/minikube-linux-amd64
   ```
3. ```
   sudo       install       minikube-linux-amd64
   /usr/local/bin/minikube
   ```
4. **Start Minikube**
5. ```
   minikube start
   ```
6. **Deploy an Application**
7. ```
   kubectl create deployment hello-minikube --
   image=k8s.gcr.io/echoserver:1.4
   ```
8. ```
   kubectl expose deployment hello-minikube --
   type=NodePort --port=8080
   ```
9. **Access the Application**
10. ```
    minikube service hello-minikube
    ```

Minikube provides an easy way to develop and test Kubernetes applications locally before moving to a production environment.

Conclusion

Kubernetes is a powerful platform for managing containerized applications at scale. Understanding its core components—Pods, Services, and Deployments—lays the foundation for efficient container orchestration. By using Minikube, developers can experiment with Kubernetes locally before deploying applications in cloud environments.

Chapter 10: Advanced Docker Topics

Docker Swarm for Container Orchestration

Docker Swarm is a native clustering and orchestration tool for Docker, allowing you to manage a cluster of Docker nodes as a single system. Unlike Kubernetes, which is more complex, Docker Swarm offers a simpler alternative for orchestrating containers.

Setting Up a Swarm Cluster

1. **Initialize the Swarm**
2. `docker swarm init --advertise-addr <MANAGER-IP>`
3. **Add Worker Nodes**
4. `docker swarm join --token <TOKEN> <MANAGER-IP>:2377`
5. **Deploy a Service**
6. `docker service create --name web --replicas 3 -p 80:80 nginx`

Scaling Services

To scale up a service:

```
docker service scale web=5
```

To remove a service:

```
docker service rm web
```

Multi-Stage Builds for Production-Ready Images

Multi-stage builds optimize Docker images by reducing the final image size and improving security.

Example: Building a Go Application

```
# Stage 1: Build the application
FROM golang:1.18 AS builder
WORKDIR /app
COPY . .
RUN go build -o myapp

# Stage 2: Create a minimal runtime image
FROM alpine:latest
WORKDIR /root/
COPY --from=builder /app/myapp .
CMD ["./myapp"]
```

Benefits:

- **Smaller Image Size**: Unused dependencies from the build stage are removed.
- **Security**: The final image contains only necessary files.
- **Improved Performance**: Smaller images lead to faster deployment.

CI/CD Pipelines with Docker (GitHub Actions, GitLab CI/CD)

GitHub Actions Example

A simple GitHub Actions workflow for building and pushing a Docker image:

```
name: Docker CI/CD
on:
  push:
    branches:
      - main

jobs:
  build:
    runs-on: ubuntu-latest
    steps:
      - name: Checkout Code
        uses: actions/checkout@v2
      - name: Login to Docker Hub
        run: echo "${{ secrets.DOCKER_PASSWORD }}"
| docker login -u "${{ secrets.DOCKER_USERNAME }}"
--password-stdin
      - name: Build and Push Image
        run: |
          docker build -t myrepo/myimage:latest .
          docker push myrepo/myimage:latest
```

GitLab CI/CD Example

```
stages:
  - build
  - deploy

docker-build:
```

```
stage: build
script:
    -          docker          build          -t
registry.gitlab.com/myrepo/myimage:latest .
    -                docker                push
registry.gitlab.com/myrepo/myimage:latest
```

Monitoring Docker Containers with Prometheus and Grafana

Installing Prometheus

1. **Create a Prometheus configuration file (`prometheus.yml`)**
2. `scrape_configs:`
3. `  - job_name: 'docker'`
4. `    static_configs:`
5. `      - targets: ['localhost:9323']`
6. **Run Prometheus as a container**
7. `docker run -d -p 9090:9090 -v $(pwd)/prometheus.yml:/etc/prometheus/prometheus.yml prom/prometheus`

Setting Up Grafana

1. **Run Grafana container**
2. `docker run -d -p 3000:3000 grafana/grafana`
3. **Connect Prometheus as a data source in Grafana**
   - Open Grafana at `http://localhost:3000`
   - Navigate to **Configuration > Data Sources**
   - Add **Prometheus** and set the URL to `http://localhost:9090`

o Save and create dashboards for container metrics

This chapter covers essential advanced Docker topics that will help you deploy and manage production-ready containerized applications efficiently.

Chapter 11: Real-World Project: Deploying a Full-Stack Application

In this chapter, we will go through the process of deploying a full-stack application using Docker. We will cover the following:

- Setting up a backend using Node.js or Python.
- Running a frontend (React, Vue, or Angular) in a container.
- Configuring a database in Docker (PostgreSQL, MySQL, or MongoDB).
- Deploying the entire application using Docker Compose.

By the end of this chapter, you will have a fully containerized application running smoothly across multiple services.

1. Setting Up the Backend

For this guide, we will use Node.js with Express.js. If you prefer Python, you can use Flask or FastAPI.

Node.js Backend

Create a new directory for the backend and initialize a Node.js project:

```
mkdir backend && cd backend
npm init -y
```

Install Express.js:

```
npm install express cors dotenv
```

Create an `index.js` file with the following content:

```
const express = require("express");
const cors = require("cors");
const app = express();

app.use(cors());
app.use(express.json());

app.get("/api", (req, res) => {
    res.json({ message: "Hello from backend!" });
});

const PORT = process.env.PORT || 5000;
app.listen(PORT, () => {
    console.log(`Server is running on port ${PORT}`);
});
```

Create a `Dockerfile` for the backend:

```
FROM node:18
WORKDIR /app
COPY package.json .
RUN npm install
COPY . .
EXPOSE 5000
CMD ["node", "index.js"]
```

Python Backend (Flask Alternative)

If you prefer Python, install Flask:

```
mkdir backend && cd backend
python -m venv venv
source venv/bin/activate
pip install flask
```

Create an `app.py` file:

```
from flask import Flask, jsonify

app = Flask(__name__)

@app.route("/api")
def home():
    return  jsonify({"message":  "Hello  from
backend!"})

if __name__ == "__main__":
    app.run(host="0.0.0.0", port=5000)
```

Create a `Dockerfile` for Flask:

```
FROM python:3.10
WORKDIR /app
COPY requirements.txt .
RUN pip install -r requirements.txt
COPY . .
EXPOSE 5000
CMD ["python", "app.py"]
```

2. Setting Up the Frontend

We will use React for the frontend, but the same process applies to Vue or Angular.

React Frontend

Create a new React app:

```
npx create-react-app frontend
cd frontend
```

Modify `src/App.js` to fetch data from the backend:

```
import { useEffect, useState } from "react";

function App() {
    const [message, setMessage] = useState("");

    useEffect(() => {
        fetch("http://localhost:5000/api")
            .then(response => response.json())
            .then(data                                =>
setMessage(data.message));
    }, []);

    return <h1>{message}</h1>;
}

export default App;
```

Create a `Dockerfile` for the frontend:

```
FROM node:18
WORKDIR /app
COPY package.json .
```

```
RUN npm install          ·
COPY . .
EXPOSE 3000
CMD ["npm", "start"]
```

3. Setting Up the Database

We will use PostgreSQL for this example.

Create a `docker-compose.yml` file:

```yaml
version: '3.8'

services:
  backend:
    build: ./backend
    ports:
      - "5000:5000"
    depends_on:
      - db

  frontend:
    build: ./frontend
    ports:
      - "3000:3000"
    depends_on:
      - backend

  db:
    image: postgres:latest
    environment:
      POSTGRES_USER: user
      POSTGRES_PASSWORD: password
      POSTGRES_DB: mydatabase
    ports:
      - "5432:5432"
    volumes:
      - pgdata:/var/lib/postgresql/data
```

```
volumes:
  pgdata:
```

4. Deploying with Docker Compose

To start all services, run:

```
docker-compose up --build
```

Your application should now be running, with the frontend available at `http://localhost:3000` and the backend at `http://localhost:5000`.

Conclusion

In this chapter, we successfully deployed a full-stack application using Docker and Docker Compose. You now have a fully containerized environment that can be easily deployed anywhere!

Conclusion and Future of Docker

Best Practices for Containerized Applications

As you move forward with Docker, it's essential to follow best practices to maximize efficiency, security, and scalability:

- **Optimize Image Size** – Use minimal base images like Alpine Linux and multi-stage builds to reduce image bloat.
- **Security First** – Regularly update images, scan for vulnerabilities, and implement least privilege access control.
- **Efficient Networking** – Use appropriate networking modes, avoid unnecessary exposure of ports, and configure internal communication properly.
- **Persistent Data Management** – Leverage volumes and bind mounts for data persistence and ensure proper backup strategies.
- **Monitoring & Logging** – Implement logging with tools like Fluentd, ELK Stack, or Prometheus for better visibility.
- **Scalability & Orchestration** – Consider Kubernetes or Docker Swarm to scale your applications dynamically.

Trends in Containerization and Cloud-Native Development

The landscape of containerization continues to evolve, driven by advancements in cloud-native technologies:

- **Kubernetes Dominance** – Kubernetes has become the de facto standard for container orchestration, offering better scalability and automation.
- **Serverless Containers** – Platforms like AWS Fargate and Google Cloud Run simplify deployment without managing infrastructure.
- **Edge Computing & IoT** – Containers are increasingly used for edge computing, bringing applications closer to users.
- **AI & Machine Learning Workloads** – Containers are now being used to deploy and scale ML models efficiently.
- **Enhanced Security Measures** – More emphasis on zero-trust architectures, runtime protection, and supply chain security in containerized environments.

Next Steps: Exploring Kubernetes, Serverless, and DevOps Tools

Now that you have mastered Docker, the next logical steps in your learning journey include:

- **Kubernetes (K8s):** Learn how to orchestrate, scale, and manage containerized applications efficiently.
- **Serverless Computing:** Explore how services like AWS Lambda, Google Cloud Functions, and Knative simplify deployments.

- **CI/CD Pipelines:** Implement DevOps best practices using GitHub Actions, Jenkins, or GitLab CI/CD with Docker.
- **Infrastructure as Code (IaC):** Discover how Terraform and Helm can automate and manage infrastructure.
- **Advanced Container Security:** Dive deeper into security best practices using tools like Trivy, Falco, and AppArmor.

By embracing these technologies, you'll stay ahead in the ever-evolving world of cloud-native development. Keep building, experimenting, and innovating!

Table of Contents

Chapter 1: Introduction to Docker 1

What is Docker? 1

Why Use Docker? 1

    1. Portability and Consistency 2

    2. Efficiency and Performance 2

    3. Scalability and Flexibility 2

    4. Simplified Deployment 2

    5. Security and Isolation 3

Docker vs. Virtual Machines 3

Installing Docker on Windows, macOS, and Linux 3

    Installing Docker on Windows 4

    Installing Docker on macOS 4

    Installing Docker on Linux (Ubuntu/Debian) 4

    Post-Installation Test 5

Chapter 2: Understanding Docker Basics 6

Key Docker Concepts: Containers, Images, and Volumes 6

    Containers 6

    Images 6

    Volumes 7

Running Your First Container 7

Exploring Docker Hub and Pulling Images 8

Understanding `docker ps`, `docker stop`, and `docker rm` 8

    Listing Running Containers (`docker ps`) 8

Stopping a Container (`docker stop`)..9

Removing a Container (`docker rm`) 9

Summary...10

Chapter 3: Docker Images and Dockerfiles 11

What are Docker Images?...11

Creating a Dockerfile...12

Basic Structure of a Dockerfile..12

Common Dockerfile Instructions...12

Building Custom Images (docker build)..13

Building an Image..13

Listing Images 13

Best Practices for Writing Dockerfiles 14

Optimizing Image Size 15

Chapter 4: Docker Networking...16

Default Networking Modes 16

1. Bridge Network (default)..16

2. Host Network...16

3. None Network..17

4. Overlay Network (Swarm mode)..17

5. Macvlan Network 17

Creating Custom Networks...18

Create a Custom Bridge Network 18

Run a Container in the Custom Network 18

Inspect a Network 18

Connecting Multiple Containers 19

Example: Running Two Containers in the Same Network 19

Exposing and Publishing Ports 19

Exposing Ports Internally...19

Publishing Ports with -p 19

Binding to a Specific IP Address 20

Summary..20

Chapter 5: Docker Volumes and Persistent Storage 21

Understanding Volumes and Bind Mounts.......................21

Volumes...21

Bind Mounts 22

Key Differences Between Volumes and Bind Mounts 22

Managing Data Between Container Restarts 23

Best Practices for Handling Databases in Containers 23

1. Always Use Volumes for Databases..........................24

2. Backup and Restore Data......................................24

3. Use --tmpfs for Temporary Data..........................24

4. Manage Volume Lifecycle.....................................24

Conclusion 25

Chapter 6: Docker Compose: Multi-Container Applications.................26

What is Docker Compose? 26

Key Features of Docker Compose: 26

Writing a docker-compose.yml File.........................27

Explanation:..27

Running Multiple Services with docker-compose up.............28

Starting Services: 28

Viewing Running Services: 28

Stopping Services: 29

Environment Variables and Configuration Management...................29

    Inline Environment Variables:..29

    `.env` File:...29

    Benefits of Using `.env`:...30

Chapter 7: Working with Docker Registries.............................31

    7.1 Introduction to Docker Registries.....................................31

    7.2 Pushing and Pulling Images to Docker Hub 31

        7.2.1 Logging into Docker Hub 32

        7.2.2 Pulling an Image from Docker Hub 32

        7.2.3 Tagging an Image 32

        7.2.4 Pushing an Image to Docker Hub 32

    7.3 Setting Up a Private Docker Registry 33

        7.3.1 Running a Local Docker Registry............................33

        7.3.2 Tagging and Pushing an Image to Your Private Registry 33

    7.4 Using Cloud-Based Registries 34

        7.4.1 Amazon Elastic Container Registry (ECR)..............34

        7.4.2 Google Container Registry (GCR).............................35

        7.4.3 GitHub Container Registry (GHCR)..........................35

    7.5 Conclusion 36

Chapter 8: Docker Security Best Practices 37

    Running Containers with Least Privilege 37

        Best Practices:..37

    Scanning Images for Vulnerabilities......................................38

        Best Practices:..38

    Limiting Container Resources 39

        Best Practices:..39

Avoiding Common Security Pitfalls...39

Best Practices:...39

Chapter 9: Introduction to Kubernetes...41

What is Kubernetes, and Why is it Important? 41

Why Kubernetes Matters 41

Deploying Docker Containers on Kubernetes...............................42

Steps to Deploy a Docker Container on Kubernetes....................42

Understanding Pods, Services, and Deployments.........................43

Pods 43

Services...43

Deployments...43

Using Minikube to Test Locally 44

Setting Up Minikube..44

Conclusion 45

Chapter 10: Advanced Docker Topics..46

Docker Swarm for Container Orchestration 46

Setting Up a Swarm Cluster..46

Scaling Services..46

Multi-Stage Builds for Production-Ready Images.......................47

Example: Building a Go Application...47

CI/CD Pipelines with Docker (GitHub Actions, GitLab CI/CD)........48

GitHub Actions Example 48

GitLab CI/CD Example 48

Monitoring Docker Containers with Prometheus and Grafana 49

Installing Prometheus 49

Setting Up Grafana 49

Chapter 11: Real-World Project: Deploying a Full-Stack Application...51

1. Setting Up the Backend 51

Node.js Backend 51

Python Backend (Flask Alternative) 53

2. Setting Up the Frontend..54

React Frontend...54

3. Setting Up the Database..55

4. Deploying with Docker Compose..56

Conclusion 56

Conclusion and Future of Docker 57

Best Practices for Containerized Applications.................................57

Trends in Containerization and Cloud-Native Development..........57

Next Steps: Exploring Kubernetes, Serverless, and DevOps Tools 58